50 Italian Risotto Recipes for Home

By: Kelly Johnson

Table of Contents

- Roasted Vegetable Risotto
- Spinach and Feta Risotto
- Roasted Butternut Squash Risotto
- Porcini and Thyme Risotto
- Zucchini Blossom Risotto
- Roasted Beet Risotto with Goat Cheese
- Lemon and Parmesan Risotto
- Mushroom and Leek Risotto
- Smoked Gouda and Asparagus Risotto
- Sun-Dried Tomato and Basil Ris
- otto
- Cherry Tomato and Basil Risotto
- Pancetta and Mushroom Risotto
- Crab and Asparagus Risotto
- Roasted Eggplant Risotto
- Creamy Parmesan Risotto

Classic Risotto Milanese

Ingredients:

- 1 1/2 cups Arborio rice
- 4 cups chicken or vegetable broth
- 1 small onion, finely chopped
- 2 tablespoons unsalted butter
- 1/2 cup dry white wine
- 1/2 teaspoon saffron threads
- 1/2 cup grated Parmesan cheese, plus extra for serving
- Salt and pepper, to taste
- Fresh parsley, chopped (for garnish, optional)

Instructions:

1. In a small saucepan, heat the chicken or vegetable broth over low heat. Keep it warm while you prepare the risotto.
2. In a separate large skillet or saucepan, melt the butter over medium heat. Add the chopped onion and cook until softened and translucent, about 5 minutes.
3. Add the Arborio rice to the skillet and stir to coat the grains with the melted butter. Cook for 2-3 minutes, stirring constantly, until the rice becomes slightly translucent around the edges.
4. Pour in the white wine and cook, stirring constantly, until the wine is absorbed by the rice.
5. Dissolve the saffron threads in a couple of tablespoons of warm water. Add the saffron-infused water to the skillet with the rice and stir well to distribute the color evenly.
6. Begin adding the warm broth to the skillet, one ladleful at a time, stirring constantly and allowing each addition of broth to be absorbed by the rice before adding more. Continue this process until the rice is cooked through and creamy, but still slightly firm to the bite (al dente). This should take about 18-20 minutes.
7. Stir in the grated Parmesan cheese until melted and well incorporated. Season with salt and pepper to taste.
8. Remove the skillet from the heat and let the risotto rest for a minute or two before serving.
9. Serve the Risotto Milanese hot, garnished with additional grated Parmesan cheese and chopped fresh parsley if desired.

Enjoy your homemade Classic Risotto Milanese as a comforting and elegant Italian dish!

Mushroom Risotto with Parmesan

Ingredients:

- 1 1/2 cups Arborio rice
- 4 cups chicken or vegetable broth
- 2 tablespoons olive oil
- 2 tablespoons unsalted butter
- 1 small onion, finely chopped
- 2 cloves garlic, minced
- 8 ounces mixed mushrooms (such as cremini, shiitake, or oyster), sliced
- 1/2 cup dry white wine
- 1/2 cup grated Parmesan cheese, plus extra for serving
- Salt and pepper, to taste
- Fresh parsley, chopped (for garnish, optional)

Instructions:

1. In a small saucepan, heat the chicken or vegetable broth over low heat. Keep it warm while you prepare the risotto.
2. In a large skillet or saucepan, heat the olive oil and butter over medium heat. Add the chopped onion and cook until softened and translucent, about 5 minutes.
3. Add the minced garlic to the skillet and cook for an additional 1-2 minutes, until fragrant.
4. Add the sliced mushrooms to the skillet and cook, stirring occasionally, until they are golden brown and tender, about 8-10 minutes.
5. Stir in the Arborio rice and cook for 1-2 minutes, stirring constantly, until the rice is well coated with the oil and butter.
6. Pour in the white wine and cook, stirring constantly, until the wine is absorbed by the rice.
7. Begin adding the warm broth to the skillet, one ladleful at a time, stirring constantly and allowing each addition of broth to be absorbed by the rice before adding more. Continue this process until the rice is cooked through and creamy, but still slightly firm to the bite (al dente). This should take about 18-20 minutes.
8. Stir in the grated Parmesan cheese until melted and well incorporated. Season with salt and pepper to taste.

9. Remove the skillet from the heat and let the risotto rest for a minute or two before serving.
10. Serve the Mushroom Risotto hot, garnished with additional grated Parmesan cheese and chopped fresh parsley if desired.

Enjoy your homemade Mushroom Risotto with Parmesan as a comforting and satisfying meal!

Asparagus Risotto with Lemon Zest

Ingredients:

- 1 1/2 cups Arborio rice
- 4 cups chicken or vegetable broth
- 2 tablespoons olive oil
- 2 tablespoons unsalted butter
- 1 small onion, finely chopped
- 2 cloves garlic, minced
- 1 bunch asparagus, trimmed and cut into bite-sized pieces
- 1/2 cup dry white wine
- Zest of 1 lemon
- 1/2 cup grated Parmesan cheese, plus extra for serving
- Salt and pepper, to taste
- Fresh parsley, chopped (for garnish, optional)

Instructions:

1. In a small saucepan, heat the chicken or vegetable broth over low heat. Keep it warm while you prepare the risotto.
2. In a large skillet or saucepan, heat the olive oil and butter over medium heat. Add the chopped onion and cook until softened and translucent, about 5 minutes.
3. Add the minced garlic to the skillet and cook for an additional 1-2 minutes, until fragrant.
4. Add the Arborio rice to the skillet and cook for 1-2 minutes, stirring constantly, until the rice is well coated with the oil and butter.
5. Pour in the white wine and cook, stirring constantly, until the wine is absorbed by the rice.
6. Begin adding the warm broth to the skillet, one ladleful at a time, stirring constantly and allowing each addition of broth to be absorbed by the rice before adding more. Continue this process until the rice is cooked through and creamy, but still slightly firm to the bite (al dente). This should take about 18-20 minutes.
7. Meanwhile, blanch the asparagus in boiling water for 2-3 minutes, until bright green and slightly tender. Drain and set aside.
8. Stir in the blanched asparagus and lemon zest into the risotto during the last 5 minutes of cooking, allowing the flavors to meld together.

9. Stir in the grated Parmesan cheese until melted and well incorporated. Season with salt and pepper to taste.
10. Remove the skillet from the heat and let the risotto rest for a minute or two before serving.
11. Serve the Asparagus Risotto with Lemon Zest hot, garnished with additional grated Parmesan cheese and chopped fresh parsley if desired.

Enjoy your homemade Asparagus Risotto with Lemon Zest as a bright and flavorful springtime dish!

Seafood Risotto with Shrimp and Scallops

Ingredients:

- 1 1/2 cups Arborio rice
- 4 cups seafood or chicken broth
- 2 tablespoons olive oil
- 2 tablespoons unsalted butter
- 1 small onion, finely chopped
- 2 cloves garlic, minced
- 1/2 cup dry white wine
- 8 ounces shrimp, peeled and deveined
- 8 ounces scallops
- Zest of 1 lemon
- 1/2 cup grated Parmesan cheese, plus extra for serving
- Salt and pepper, to taste
- Fresh parsley, chopped (for garnish, optional)

Instructions:

1. In a small saucepan, heat the seafood or chicken broth over low heat. Keep it warm while you prepare the risotto.
2. In a large skillet or saucepan, heat the olive oil and butter over medium heat. Add the chopped onion and cook until softened and translucent, about 5 minutes.
3. Add the minced garlic to the skillet and cook for an additional 1-2 minutes, until fragrant.
4. Add the Arborio rice to the skillet and cook for 1-2 minutes, stirring constantly, until the rice is well coated with the oil and butter.
5. Pour in the white wine and cook, stirring constantly, until the wine is absorbed by the rice.
6. Begin adding the warm broth to the skillet, one ladleful at a time, stirring constantly and allowing each addition of broth to be absorbed by the rice before adding more. Continue this process until the rice is cooked through and creamy, but still slightly firm to the bite (al dente). This should take about 18-20 minutes.
7. Meanwhile, season the shrimp and scallops with salt and pepper. In a separate skillet, heat a tablespoon of olive oil over medium-high heat. Add the shrimp and

scallops and cook for 2-3 minutes on each side, until they are cooked through and lightly browned. Remove from heat and set aside.

8. Stir in the lemon zest into the risotto during the last 5 minutes of cooking, allowing the flavors to meld together.
9. Stir in the grated Parmesan cheese until melted and well incorporated. Season with salt and pepper to taste.
10. Remove the skillet from the heat and gently fold in the cooked shrimp and scallops.
11. Let the risotto rest for a minute or two before serving.
12. Serve the Seafood Risotto with Shrimp and Scallops hot, garnished with additional grated Parmesan cheese and chopped fresh parsley if desired.

Enjoy your homemade Seafood Risotto with Shrimp and Scallops as an elegant and indulgent meal!

Butternut Squash Risotto with Sage

Ingredients:

- 1 small butternut squash, peeled, seeded, and diced
- 4 cups vegetable or chicken broth
- 2 tablespoons olive oil
- 2 tablespoons unsalted butter
- 1 small onion, finely chopped
- 2 cloves garlic, minced
- 1 1/2 cups Arborio rice
- 1/2 cup dry white wine
- 1/2 cup grated Parmesan cheese
- 2 tablespoons fresh sage leaves, chopped
- Salt and pepper, to taste
- Freshly grated nutmeg (optional)

Instructions:

1. Preheat the oven to 400°F (200°C). Place the diced butternut squash on a baking sheet lined with parchment paper. Drizzle with olive oil and season with salt and pepper. Roast in the preheated oven for 20-25 minutes, or until tender and lightly caramelized. Remove from the oven and set aside.
2. In a small saucepan, heat the vegetable or chicken broth over low heat. Keep it warm while you prepare the risotto.
3. In a large skillet or saucepan, heat the olive oil and butter over medium heat. Add the chopped onion and cook until softened and translucent, about 5 minutes.
4. Add the minced garlic to the skillet and cook for an additional 1-2 minutes, until fragrant.
5. Add the Arborio rice to the skillet and cook for 1-2 minutes, stirring constantly, until the rice is well coated with the oil and butter.
6. Pour in the white wine and cook, stirring constantly, until the wine is absorbed by the rice.
7. Begin adding the warm broth to the skillet, one ladleful at a time, stirring constantly and allowing each addition of broth to be absorbed by the rice before adding more. Continue this process until the rice is cooked through and creamy, but still slightly firm to the bite (al dente). This should take about 18-20 minutes.

8. Stir in the roasted butternut squash and fresh sage leaves during the last 5 minutes of cooking, allowing the flavors to meld together.
9. Stir in the grated Parmesan cheese until melted and well incorporated. Season with salt, pepper, and freshly grated nutmeg to taste.
10. Remove the skillet from the heat and let the risotto rest for a minute or two before serving.
11. Serve the Butternut Squash Risotto with Sage hot, garnished with additional grated Parmesan cheese and fresh sage leaves if desired.

Enjoy your homemade Butternut Squash Risotto with Sage as a comforting and delicious meal!

Spinach and Ricotta Risotto

Ingredients:

- 1 1/2 cups Arborio rice
- 4 cups vegetable or chicken broth
- 2 tablespoons olive oil
- 2 tablespoons unsalted butter
- 1 small onion, finely chopped
- 2 cloves garlic, minced
- 6 ounces fresh spinach leaves, washed and chopped
- 1/2 cup dry white wine
- 1/2 cup ricotta cheese
- 1/2 cup grated Parmesan cheese
- Salt and pepper, to taste
- Fresh parsley, chopped (for garnish, optional)

Instructions:

1. In a small saucepan, heat the vegetable or chicken broth over low heat. Keep it warm while you prepare the risotto.
2. In a large skillet or saucepan, heat the olive oil and butter over medium heat. Add the chopped onion and cook until softened and translucent, about 5 minutes.
3. Add the minced garlic to the skillet and cook for an additional 1-2 minutes, until fragrant.
4. Add the Arborio rice to the skillet and cook for 1-2 minutes, stirring constantly, until the rice is well coated with the oil and butter.
5. Pour in the white wine and cook, stirring constantly, until the wine is absorbed by the rice.
6. Begin adding the warm broth to the skillet, one ladleful at a time, stirring constantly and allowing each addition of broth to be absorbed by the rice before adding more. Continue this process until the rice is cooked through and creamy, but still slightly firm to the bite (al dente). This should take about 18-20 minutes.
7. Stir in the chopped spinach leaves during the last 5 minutes of cooking, allowing them to wilt and cook down.
8. Stir in the ricotta cheese and grated Parmesan cheese until melted and well incorporated. Season with salt and pepper to taste.

9. Remove the skillet from the heat and let the risotto rest for a minute or two before serving.
10. Serve the Spinach and Ricotta Risotto hot, garnished with chopped fresh parsley if desired.

Enjoy your homemade Spinach and Ricotta Risotto as a comforting and nutritious meal!

Tomato and Basil Risotto

Ingredients:

- 1 1/2 cups Arborio rice
- 4 cups vegetable or chicken broth
- 2 tablespoons olive oil
- 2 tablespoons unsalted butter
- 1 small onion, finely chopped
- 2 cloves garlic, minced
- 2 cups ripe tomatoes, diced
- 1/2 cup dry white wine
- 1/2 cup grated Parmesan cheese
- 1/4 cup fresh basil leaves, chopped
- Salt and pepper, to taste

Instructions:

1. In a small saucepan, heat the vegetable or chicken broth over low heat. Keep it warm while you prepare the risotto.
2. In a large skillet or saucepan, heat the olive oil and butter over medium heat. Add the chopped onion and cook until softened and translucent, about 5 minutes.
3. Add the minced garlic to the skillet and cook for an additional 1-2 minutes, until fragrant.
4. Add the Arborio rice to the skillet and cook for 1-2 minutes, stirring constantly, until the rice is well coated with the oil and butter.
5. Pour in the white wine and cook, stirring constantly, until the wine is absorbed by the rice.
6. Add the diced tomatoes to the skillet and cook for 2-3 minutes, until they begin to soften and release their juices.
7. Begin adding the warm broth to the skillet, one ladleful at a time, stirring constantly and allowing each addition of broth to be absorbed by the rice before adding more. Continue this process until the rice is cooked through and creamy, but still slightly firm to the bite (al dente). This should take about 18-20 minutes.
8. Stir in the grated Parmesan cheese until melted and well incorporated. Season with salt and pepper to taste.
9. Remove the skillet from the heat and stir in the chopped fresh basil leaves.

10. Let the risotto rest for a minute or two before serving.
11. Serve the Tomato and Basil Risotto hot, garnished with additional grated Parmesan cheese and fresh basil leaves if desired.

Enjoy your homemade Tomato and Basil Risotto as a flavorful and comforting meal!

Truffle Risotto with Parmesan

Ingredients:

- 1 1/2 cups Arborio rice
- 4 cups vegetable or chicken broth
- 2 tablespoons unsalted butter
- 2 tablespoons olive oil
- 1 small onion, finely chopped
- 2 cloves garlic, minced
- 1/2 cup dry white wine
- 2 tablespoons truffle oil
- 1/2 cup grated Parmesan cheese
- Salt and pepper, to taste
- Fresh parsley, chopped (for garnish, optional)

Instructions:

1. In a small saucepan, heat the vegetable or chicken broth over low heat. Keep it warm while you prepare the risotto.
2. In a large skillet or saucepan, heat the olive oil and butter over medium heat. Add the chopped onion and cook until softened and translucent, about 5 minutes.
3. Add the minced garlic to the skillet and cook for an additional 1-2 minutes, until fragrant.
4. Add the Arborio rice to the skillet and cook for 1-2 minutes, stirring constantly, until the rice is well coated with the oil and butter.
5. Pour in the white wine and cook, stirring constantly, until the wine is absorbed by the rice.
6. Begin adding the warm broth to the skillet, one ladleful at a time, stirring constantly and allowing each addition of broth to be absorbed by the rice before adding more. Continue this process until the rice is cooked through and creamy, but still slightly firm to the bite (al dente). This should take about 18-20 minutes.
7. Stir in the truffle oil and grated Parmesan cheese until melted and well incorporated. Season with salt and pepper to taste.
8. Remove the skillet from the heat and let the risotto rest for a minute or two before serving.

9. Serve the Truffle Risotto with Parmesan hot, garnished with chopped fresh parsley if desired.

Enjoy your homemade Truffle Risotto with Parmesan as a decadent and elegant dish!

Roasted Red Pepper Risotto

Ingredients:

- 2 large red bell peppers
- 4 cups vegetable or chicken broth
- 2 tablespoons olive oil
- 2 tablespoons unsalted butter
- 1 small onion, finely chopped
- 2 cloves garlic, minced
- 1 1/2 cups Arborio rice
- 1/2 cup dry white wine
- 1/2 cup grated Parmesan cheese
- Salt and pepper, to taste
- Fresh basil leaves, chopped (for garnish, optional)

Instructions:

1. Preheat the oven to 400°F (200°C). Place the whole red bell peppers on a baking sheet lined with parchment paper. Roast in the preheated oven for 20-25 minutes, or until the peppers are charred and softened. Remove from the oven and let cool slightly. Once cooled, peel off the skin, remove the seeds and stems, and chop the flesh into small pieces.
2. In a small saucepan, heat the vegetable or chicken broth over low heat. Keep it warm while you prepare the risotto.
3. In a large skillet or saucepan, heat the olive oil and butter over medium heat. Add the chopped onion and cook until softened and translucent, about 5 minutes.
4. Add the minced garlic to the skillet and cook for an additional 1-2 minutes, until fragrant.
5. Add the Arborio rice to the skillet and cook for 1-2 minutes, stirring constantly, until the rice is well coated with the oil and butter.
6. Pour in the white wine and cook, stirring constantly, until the wine is absorbed by the rice.
7. Begin adding the warm broth to the skillet, one ladleful at a time, stirring constantly and allowing each addition of broth to be absorbed by the rice before adding more. Continue this process until the rice is cooked through and creamy, but still slightly firm to the bite (al dente). This should take about 18-20 minutes.

8. Stir in the chopped roasted red peppers during the last 5 minutes of cooking, allowing them to warm through and infuse their flavor into the risotto.
9. Stir in the grated Parmesan cheese until melted and well incorporated. Season with salt and pepper to taste.
10. Remove the skillet from the heat and let the risotto rest for a minute or two before serving.
11. Serve the Roasted Red Pepper Risotto hot, garnished with chopped fresh basil leaves if desired.

Enjoy your homemade Roasted Red Pepper Risotto as a delicious and comforting meal!

Saffron Risotto with Peas

Ingredients:

- 1 1/2 cups Arborio rice
- 4 cups vegetable or chicken broth
- 2 tablespoons olive oil
- 2 tablespoons unsalted butter
- 1 small onion, finely chopped
- 2 cloves garlic, minced
- 1/2 cup dry white wine
- 1/2 teaspoon saffron threads
- 1 cup frozen peas, thawed
- 1/2 cup grated Parmesan cheese
- Salt and pepper, to taste
- Fresh parsley, chopped (for garnish, optional)

Instructions:

1. In a small saucepan, heat the vegetable or chicken broth over low heat. Add the saffron threads to the warm broth and let it steep for 10-15 minutes to infuse the flavor and color.
2. In a large skillet or saucepan, heat the olive oil and butter over medium heat. Add the chopped onion and cook until softened and translucent, about 5 minutes.
3. Add the minced garlic to the skillet and cook for an additional 1-2 minutes, until fragrant.
4. Add the Arborio rice to the skillet and cook for 1-2 minutes, stirring constantly, until the rice is well coated with the oil and butter.
5. Pour in the white wine and cook, stirring constantly, until the wine is absorbed by the rice.
6. Begin adding the warm saffron-infused broth to the skillet, one ladleful at a time, stirring constantly and allowing each addition of broth to be absorbed by the rice before adding more. Continue this process until the rice is cooked through and creamy, but still slightly firm to the bite (al dente). This should take about 18-20 minutes.
7. Stir in the thawed peas during the last 5 minutes of cooking, allowing them to warm through.

8. Stir in the grated Parmesan cheese until melted and well incorporated. Season with salt and pepper to taste.
9. Remove the skillet from the heat and let the risotto rest for a minute or two before serving.
10. Serve the Saffron Risotto with Peas hot, garnished with chopped fresh parsley if desired.

Enjoy your homemade Saffron Risotto with Peas as a flavorful and elegant dish!

Gorgonzola and Walnut Risotto

Ingredients:

- 1 1/2 cups Arborio rice
- 4 cups vegetable or chicken broth
- 2 tablespoons olive oil
- 2 tablespoons unsalted butter
- 1 small onion, finely chopped
- 2 cloves garlic, minced
- 1/2 cup dry white wine
- 4 ounces Gorgonzola cheese, crumbled
- 1/2 cup walnuts, chopped and toasted
- Salt and pepper, to taste
- Fresh parsley, chopped (for garnish, optional)

Instructions:

1. In a small saucepan, heat the vegetable or chicken broth over low heat. Keep it warm while you prepare the risotto.
2. In a large skillet or saucepan, heat the olive oil and butter over medium heat. Add the chopped onion and cook until softened and translucent, about 5 minutes.
3. Add the minced garlic to the skillet and cook for an additional 1-2 minutes, until fragrant.
4. Add the Arborio rice to the skillet and cook for 1-2 minutes, stirring constantly, until the rice is well coated with the oil and butter.
5. Pour in the white wine and cook, stirring constantly, until the wine is absorbed by the rice.
6. Begin adding the warm broth to the skillet, one ladleful at a time, stirring constantly and allowing each addition of broth to be absorbed by the rice before adding more. Continue this process until the rice is cooked through and creamy, but still slightly firm to the bite (al dente). This should take about 18-20 minutes.
7. Stir in the crumbled Gorgonzola cheese until melted and well incorporated.
8. Stir in the chopped and toasted walnuts, reserving some for garnish if desired.
9. Season with salt and pepper to taste.
10. Remove the skillet from the heat and let the risotto rest for a minute or two before serving.

11. Serve the Gorgonzola and Walnut Risotto hot, garnished with additional chopped walnuts and fresh parsley if desired.

Enjoy your homemade Gorgonzola and Walnut Risotto as a decadent and satisfying dish!

Lemon Risotto with Grilled Chicken

Ingredients for Lemon Risotto:

- 1 1/2 cups Arborio rice
- 4 cups vegetable or chicken broth
- 2 tablespoons olive oil
- 2 tablespoons unsalted butter
- 1 small onion, finely chopped
- 2 cloves garlic, minced
- Zest of 2 lemons
- Juice of 1 lemon
- 1/2 cup dry white wine
- 1/2 cup grated Parmesan cheese
- Salt and pepper, to taste
- Fresh parsley, chopped (for garnish, optional)

Ingredients for Grilled Chicken:

- 2 boneless, skinless chicken breasts
- 2 tablespoons olive oil
- Salt and pepper, to taste
- Lemon wedges, for serving

Instructions:

1. Preheat the grill to medium-high heat.
2. Season the chicken breasts with olive oil, salt, and pepper.
3. Grill the chicken breasts for 6-8 minutes on each side, or until cooked through and grill marks appear. Remove from the grill and let them rest for a few minutes before slicing.
4. In the meantime, prepare the lemon risotto:
5. In a small saucepan, heat the vegetable or chicken broth over low heat. Keep it warm while you prepare the risotto.
6. In a large skillet or saucepan, heat the olive oil and butter over medium heat. Add the chopped onion and cook until softened and translucent, about 5 minutes.

7. Add the minced garlic to the skillet and cook for an additional 1-2 minutes, until fragrant.
8. Add the Arborio rice to the skillet and cook for 1-2 minutes, stirring constantly, until the rice is well coated with the oil and butter.
9. Pour in the white wine and cook, stirring constantly, until the wine is absorbed by the rice.
10. Begin adding the warm broth to the skillet, one ladleful at a time, stirring constantly and allowing each addition of broth to be absorbed by the rice before adding more. Continue this process until the rice is cooked through and creamy, but still slightly firm to the bite (al dente). This should take about 18-20 minutes.
11. Stir in the lemon zest and lemon juice until well incorporated.
12. Stir in the grated Parmesan cheese until melted and well incorporated. Season with salt and pepper to taste.
13. Remove the skillet from the heat and let the risotto rest for a minute or two before serving.
14. Serve the lemon risotto hot, garnished with chopped fresh parsley if desired, and sliced grilled chicken on top.
15. Serve with lemon wedges on the side for an extra burst of lemon flavor.

Enjoy your homemade Lemon Risotto with Grilled Chicken as a delicious and vibrant meal!

Porcini Mushroom Risotto

Ingredients:

- 1 1/2 cups Arborio rice
- 4 cups vegetable or chicken broth
- 1 ounce dried porcini mushrooms
- 2 tablespoons olive oil
- 2 tablespoons unsalted butter
- 1 small onion, finely chopped
- 2 cloves garlic, minced
- 1/2 cup dry white wine
- 1/2 cup grated Parmesan cheese
- Salt and pepper, to taste
- Fresh parsley, chopped (for garnish, optional)

Instructions:

1. In a small bowl, soak the dried porcini mushrooms in 1 cup of warm water for about 20 minutes, or until softened. Once softened, remove the mushrooms from the water, reserving the soaking liquid. Chop the rehydrated mushrooms into small pieces.
2. In a small saucepan, heat the vegetable or chicken broth over low heat. Keep it warm while you prepare the risotto.
3. In a large skillet or saucepan, heat the olive oil and butter over medium heat. Add the chopped onion and cook until softened and translucent, about 5 minutes.
4. Add the minced garlic to the skillet and cook for an additional 1-2 minutes, until fragrant.
5. Add the Arborio rice to the skillet and cook for 1-2 minutes, stirring constantly, until the rice is well coated with the oil and butter.
6. Pour in the white wine and cook, stirring constantly, until the wine is absorbed by the rice.
7. Begin adding the warm broth to the skillet, one ladleful at a time, stirring constantly and allowing each addition of broth to be absorbed by the rice before adding more.
8. In the meantime, strain the reserved soaking liquid from the porcini mushrooms through a fine-mesh sieve or cheesecloth to remove any grit. Add the strained

soaking liquid to the risotto, along with the chopped porcini mushrooms, during the cooking process.

9. Continue adding broth and stirring until the rice is cooked through and creamy, but still slightly firm to the bite (al dente). This should take about 18-20 minutes.
10. Stir in the grated Parmesan cheese until melted and well incorporated. Season with salt and pepper to taste.
11. Remove the skillet from the heat and let the risotto rest for a minute or two before serving.
12. Serve the Porcini Mushroom Risotto hot, garnished with chopped fresh parsley if desired.

Enjoy your homemade Porcini Mushroom Risotto as a flavorful and comforting dish!

Pumpkin Risotto with Pancetta

Ingredients:

- 1 1/2 cups Arborio rice
- 4 cups vegetable or chicken broth
- 1 cup pumpkin puree
- 4 ounces pancetta, diced
- 2 tablespoons olive oil
- 2 tablespoons unsalted butter
- 1 small onion, finely chopped
- 2 cloves garlic, minced
- 1/2 cup dry white wine
- 1/2 cup grated Parmesan cheese
- Salt and pepper, to taste
- Fresh sage leaves, chopped (for garnish, optional)

Instructions:

1. In a small saucepan, heat the vegetable or chicken broth over low heat. Keep it warm while you prepare the risotto.
2. In a large skillet or saucepan, heat the olive oil over medium heat. Add the diced pancetta and cook until crispy and golden brown, about 5-7 minutes. Remove the pancetta from the skillet with a slotted spoon and set aside on a paper towel-lined plate.
3. In the same skillet, add the butter and chopped onion. Cook until the onion is softened and translucent, about 5 minutes.
4. Add the minced garlic to the skillet and cook for an additional 1-2 minutes, until fragrant.
5. Add the Arborio rice to the skillet and cook for 1-2 minutes, stirring constantly, until the rice is well coated with the oil and butter.
6. Pour in the white wine and cook, stirring constantly, until the wine is absorbed by the rice.
7. Begin adding the warm broth to the skillet, one ladleful at a time, stirring constantly and allowing each addition of broth to be absorbed by the rice before adding more.
8. Stir in the pumpkin puree until well incorporated.

9. Continue adding broth and stirring until the rice is cooked through and creamy, but still slightly firm to the bite (al dente). This should take about 18-20 minutes.
10. Stir in the grated Parmesan cheese until melted and well incorporated. Season with salt and pepper to taste.
11. Remove the skillet from the heat and let the risotto rest for a minute or two before serving.
12. Serve the Pumpkin Risotto with Pancetta hot, garnished with the crispy pancetta pieces and chopped fresh sage leaves if desired.

Enjoy your homemade Pumpkin Risotto with Pancetta as a comforting and flavorful autumn meal!

Artichoke Risotto with Pecorino

Ingredients:

- 1 1/2 cups Arborio rice
- 4 cups vegetable or chicken broth
- 1 can (14 oz) artichoke hearts, drained and chopped
- 2 tablespoons olive oil
- 2 tablespoons unsalted butter
- 1 small onion, finely chopped
- 2 cloves garlic, minced
- 1/2 cup dry white wine
- 1/2 cup grated Pecorino cheese
- Salt and pepper, to taste
- Fresh parsley, chopped (for garnish, optional)

Instructions:

1. In a small saucepan, heat the vegetable or chicken broth over low heat. Keep it warm while you prepare the risotto.
2. In a large skillet or saucepan, heat the olive oil and butter over medium heat. Add the chopped onion and cook until softened and translucent, about 5 minutes.
3. Add the minced garlic to the skillet and cook for an additional 1-2 minutes, until fragrant.
4. Add the Arborio rice to the skillet and cook for 1-2 minutes, stirring constantly, until the rice is well coated with the oil and butter.
5. Pour in the white wine and cook, stirring constantly, until the wine is absorbed by the rice.
6. Begin adding the warm broth to the skillet, one ladleful at a time, stirring constantly and allowing each addition of broth to be absorbed by the rice before adding more.
7. Stir in the chopped artichoke hearts during the last 5 minutes of cooking, allowing them to warm through.
8. Continue adding broth and stirring until the rice is cooked through and creamy, but still slightly firm to the bite (al dente). This should take about 18-20 minutes.
9. Stir in the grated Pecorino cheese until melted and well incorporated. Season with salt and pepper to taste.

10. Remove the skillet from the heat and let the risotto rest for a minute or two before serving.
11. Serve the Artichoke Risotto with Pecorino hot, garnished with chopped fresh parsley if desired.

Enjoy your homemade Artichoke Risotto with Pecorino as a flavorful and satisfying dish!

Spring Vegetable Risotto

Ingredients:

- 1 1/2 cups Arborio rice
- 4 cups vegetable or chicken broth
- 2 tablespoons olive oil
- 2 tablespoons unsalted butter
- 1 small onion, finely chopped
- 2 cloves garlic, minced
- 1 cup asparagus, trimmed and cut into 1-inch pieces
- 1 cup fresh peas (or thawed frozen peas)
- 1 cup cherry tomatoes, halved
- Zest of 1 lemon
- 1/2 cup dry white wine
- 1/2 cup grated Parmesan cheese
- Salt and pepper, to taste
- Fresh basil leaves, chopped (for garnish, optional)

Instructions:

1. In a small saucepan, heat the vegetable or chicken broth over low heat. Keep it warm while you prepare the risotto.
2. In a large skillet or saucepan, heat the olive oil and butter over medium heat. Add the chopped onion and cook until softened and translucent, about 5 minutes.
3. Add the minced garlic to the skillet and cook for an additional 1-2 minutes, until fragrant.
4. Add the Arborio rice to the skillet and cook for 1-2 minutes, stirring constantly, until the rice is well coated with the oil and butter.
5. Pour in the white wine and cook, stirring constantly, until the wine is absorbed by the rice.
6. Begin adding the warm broth to the skillet, one ladleful at a time, stirring constantly and allowing each addition of broth to be absorbed by the rice before adding more.
7. About halfway through the cooking process (after about 10 minutes), stir in the asparagus pieces and peas.

8. Continue adding broth and stirring until the rice is cooked through and creamy, but still slightly firm to the bite (al dente). This should take about 18-20 minutes in total.
9. Stir in the halved cherry tomatoes and lemon zest during the last 5 minutes of cooking, allowing them to warm through.
10. Stir in the grated Parmesan cheese until melted and well incorporated. Season with salt and pepper to taste.
11. Remove the skillet from the heat and let the risotto rest for a minute or two before serving.
12. Serve the Spring Vegetable Risotto hot, garnished with chopped fresh basil leaves if desired.

Enjoy your homemade Spring Vegetable Risotto as a light and flavorful dish perfect for the season!

Beetroot Risotto with Goat Cheese

Ingredients:

- 1 1/2 cups Arborio rice
- 4 cups vegetable or chicken broth
- 2 tablespoons olive oil
- 2 tablespoons unsalted butter
- 1 small onion, finely chopped
- 2 cloves garlic, minced
- 2 medium-sized beetroots, peeled and grated
- 1/2 cup dry white wine
- 4 ounces goat cheese, crumbled
- Salt and pepper, to taste
- Fresh parsley, chopped (for garnish, optional)

Instructions:

1. In a small saucepan, heat the vegetable or chicken broth over low heat. Keep it warm while you prepare the risotto.
2. In a large skillet or saucepan, heat the olive oil and butter over medium heat. Add the chopped onion and cook until softened and translucent, about 5 minutes.
3. Add the minced garlic to the skillet and cook for an additional 1-2 minutes, until fragrant.
4. Add the grated beetroots to the skillet and cook for 3-4 minutes, stirring occasionally, until they start to soften.
5. Add the Arborio rice to the skillet and cook for 1-2 minutes, stirring constantly, until the rice is well coated with the oil and butter.
6. Pour in the white wine and cook, stirring constantly, until the wine is absorbed by the rice.
7. Begin adding the warm broth to the skillet, one ladleful at a time, stirring constantly and allowing each addition of broth to be absorbed by the rice before adding more.
8. Continue adding broth and stirring until the rice is cooked through and creamy, but still slightly firm to the bite (al dente). This should take about 18-20 minutes.
9. Stir in the crumbled goat cheese until melted and well incorporated. Season with salt and pepper to taste.

10. Remove the skillet from the heat and let the risotto rest for a minute or two before serving.
11. Serve the Beetroot Risotto with Goat Cheese hot, garnished with chopped fresh parsley if desired.

Enjoy your homemade Beetroot Risotto with Goat Cheese as a vibrant and delicious meal!

Green Pea Risotto with Mint

Ingredients:

- 1 1/2 cups Arborio rice
- 4 cups vegetable or chicken broth
- 2 tablespoons olive oil
- 2 tablespoons unsalted butter
- 1 small onion, finely chopped
- 2 cloves garlic, minced
- 2 cups fresh or frozen green peas
- 1/2 cup dry white wine
- 1/4 cup fresh mint leaves, chopped
- 1/2 cup grated Parmesan cheese
- Salt and pepper, to taste
- Fresh mint leaves, for garnish

Instructions:

1. In a small saucepan, heat the vegetable or chicken broth over low heat. Keep it warm while you prepare the risotto.
2. In a large skillet or saucepan, heat the olive oil and butter over medium heat. Add the chopped onion and cook until softened and translucent, about 5 minutes.
3. Add the minced garlic to the skillet and cook for an additional 1-2 minutes, until fragrant.
4. Add the Arborio rice to the skillet and cook for 1-2 minutes, stirring constantly, until the rice is well coated with the oil and butter.
5. Pour in the white wine and cook, stirring constantly, until the wine is absorbed by the rice.
6. Begin adding the warm broth to the skillet, one ladleful at a time, stirring constantly and allowing each addition of broth to be absorbed by the rice before adding more.
7. About halfway through the cooking process (after about 10 minutes), stir in the green peas.
8. Continue adding broth and stirring until the rice is cooked through and creamy, but still slightly firm to the bite (al dente). This should take about 18-20 minutes in total.

9. Stir in the chopped fresh mint leaves during the last 5 minutes of cooking, allowing them to infuse their flavor into the risotto.
10. Stir in the grated Parmesan cheese until melted and well incorporated. Season with salt and pepper to taste.
11. Remove the skillet from the heat and let the risotto rest for a minute or two before serving.
12. Serve the Green Pea Risotto with Mint hot, garnished with fresh mint leaves.

Enjoy your homemade Green Pea Risotto with Mint as a light and flavorful dish!

Radicchio and Gorgonzola Risotto

Ingredients:

- 1 1/2 cups Arborio rice
- 4 cups vegetable or chicken broth
- 2 tablespoons olive oil
- 2 tablespoons unsalted butter
- 1 small onion, finely chopped
- 2 cloves garlic, minced
- 1 small head of radicchio, thinly sliced
- 1/2 cup dry white wine
- 4 ounces Gorgonzola cheese, crumbled
- Salt and pepper, to taste
- Fresh parsley, chopped (for garnish, optional)

Instructions:

1. In a small saucepan, heat the vegetable or chicken broth over low heat. Keep it warm while you prepare the risotto.
2. In a large skillet or saucepan, heat the olive oil and butter over medium heat. Add the chopped onion and cook until softened and translucent, about 5 minutes.
3. Add the minced garlic to the skillet and cook for an additional 1-2 minutes, until fragrant.
4. Add the sliced radicchio to the skillet and cook for 5-7 minutes, stirring occasionally, until wilted and tender.
5. Add the Arborio rice to the skillet and cook for 1-2 minutes, stirring constantly, until the rice is well coated with the oil and butter.
6. Pour in the white wine and cook, stirring constantly, until the wine is absorbed by the rice.
7. Begin adding the warm broth to the skillet, one ladleful at a time, stirring constantly and allowing each addition of broth to be absorbed by the rice before adding more.
8. Continue adding broth and stirring until the rice is cooked through and creamy, but still slightly firm to the bite (al dente). This should take about 18-20 minutes.
9. Stir in the crumbled Gorgonzola cheese until melted and well incorporated. Season with salt and pepper to taste.

10. Remove the skillet from the heat and let the risotto rest for a minute or two before serving.
11. Serve the Radicchio and Gorgonzola Risotto hot, garnished with chopped fresh parsley if desired.

Enjoy your homemade Radicchio and Gorgonzola Risotto as a bold and delicious meal!

Roasted Tomato Risotto

Ingredients:

- 1 1/2 cups Arborio rice
- 4 cups vegetable or chicken broth
- 2 tablespoons olive oil
- 2 tablespoons unsalted butter
- 1 small onion, finely chopped
- 2 cloves garlic, minced
- 2 cups cherry tomatoes, halved
- 2 tablespoons balsamic vinegar
- Salt and pepper, to taste
- 1/2 cup dry white wine
- 1/2 cup grated Parmesan cheese
- Fresh basil leaves, chopped (for garnish, optional)

Instructions:

1. Preheat your oven to 400°F (200°C).
2. Place the halved cherry tomatoes on a baking sheet lined with parchment paper. Drizzle with olive oil and balsamic vinegar, and season with salt and pepper. Toss to coat evenly.
3. Roast the tomatoes in the preheated oven for about 20-25 minutes, or until they are soft and slightly caramelized. Remove from the oven and set aside.
4. In a small saucepan, heat the vegetable or chicken broth over low heat. Keep it warm while you prepare the risotto.
5. In a large skillet or saucepan, heat the olive oil and butter over medium heat. Add the chopped onion and cook until softened and translucent, about 5 minutes.
6. Add the minced garlic to the skillet and cook for an additional 1-2 minutes, until fragrant.
7. Add the Arborio rice to the skillet and cook for 1-2 minutes, stirring constantly, until the rice is well coated with the oil and butter.
8. Pour in the white wine and cook, stirring constantly, until the wine is absorbed by the rice.

9. Begin adding the warm broth to the skillet, one ladleful at a time, stirring constantly and allowing each addition of broth to be absorbed by the rice before adding more.

10. Continue adding broth and stirring until the rice is cooked through and creamy, but still slightly firm to the bite (al dente). This should take about 18-20 minutes.

11. Stir in the roasted cherry tomatoes, along with any juices from the baking sheet.

12. Stir in the grated Parmesan cheese until melted and well incorporated. Season with salt and pepper to taste.

13. Remove the skillet from the heat and let the risotto rest for a minute or two before serving.

14. Serve the Roasted Tomato Risotto hot, garnished with chopped fresh basil leaves if desired.

Enjoy your homemade Roasted Tomato Risotto as a flavorful and comforting meal!

Lemon Asparagus Risotto

Ingredients:

- 1 1/2 cups Arborio rice
- 4 cups vegetable or chicken broth
- 2 tablespoons olive oil
- 2 tablespoons unsalted butter
- 1 small onion, finely chopped
- 2 cloves garlic, minced
- 1 bunch asparagus, trimmed and cut into bite-sized pieces
- Zest of 1 lemon
- Juice of 1 lemon
- 1/2 cup dry white wine
- 1/2 cup grated Parmesan cheese
- Salt and pepper, to taste
- Fresh parsley, chopped (for garnish, optional)

Instructions:

1. In a small saucepan, heat the vegetable or chicken broth over low heat. Keep it warm while you prepare the risotto.
2. In a large skillet or saucepan, heat the olive oil and butter over medium heat. Add the chopped onion and cook until softened and translucent, about 5 minutes.
3. Add the minced garlic to the skillet and cook for an additional 1-2 minutes, until fragrant.
4. Add the Arborio rice to the skillet and cook for 1-2 minutes, stirring constantly, until the rice is well coated with the oil and butter.
5. Pour in the white wine and cook, stirring constantly, until the wine is absorbed by the rice.
6. Begin adding the warm broth to the skillet, one ladleful at a time, stirring constantly and allowing each addition of broth to be absorbed by the rice before adding more.
7. About halfway through the cooking process (after about 10 minutes), stir in the asparagus pieces.
8. Continue adding broth and stirring until the rice is cooked through and creamy, but still slightly firm to the bite (al dente). This should take about 18-20 minutes.

9. Stir in the lemon zest and lemon juice until well incorporated.
10. Stir in the grated Parmesan cheese until melted and well incorporated. Season with salt and pepper to taste.
11. Remove the skillet from the heat and let the risotto rest for a minute or two before serving.
12. Serve the Lemon Asparagus Risotto hot, garnished with chopped fresh parsley if desired.

Enjoy your homemade Lemon Asparagus Risotto as a light and flavorful meal!

Pumpkin and Sage Risotto

Ingredients:

- 1 1/2 cups Arborio rice
- 4 cups vegetable or chicken broth
- 2 tablespoons olive oil
- 2 tablespoons unsalted butter
- 1 small onion, finely chopped
- 2 cloves garlic, minced
- 1 cup pumpkin puree
- 1/2 cup dry white wine
- 1/4 cup grated Parmesan cheese
- Salt and pepper, to taste
- Fresh sage leaves, chopped (for garnish, optional)

Instructions:

1. In a small saucepan, heat the vegetable or chicken broth over low heat. Keep it warm while you prepare the risotto.
2. In a large skillet or saucepan, heat the olive oil and butter over medium heat. Add the chopped onion and cook until softened and translucent, about 5 minutes.
3. Add the minced garlic to the skillet and cook for an additional 1-2 minutes, until fragrant.
4. Add the Arborio rice to the skillet and cook for 1-2 minutes, stirring constantly, until the rice is well coated with the oil and butter.
5. Pour in the white wine and cook, stirring constantly, until the wine is absorbed by the rice.
6. Begin adding the warm broth to the skillet, one ladleful at a time, stirring constantly and allowing each addition of broth to be absorbed by the rice before adding more.
7. Stir in the pumpkin puree and continue adding broth until the rice is cooked through and creamy, but still slightly firm to the bite (al dente). This should take about 18-20 minutes.
8. Stir in the grated Parmesan cheese until melted and well incorporated. Season with salt and pepper to taste.

9. Remove the skillet from the heat and let the risotto rest for a minute or two before serving.
10. Serve the Pumpkin and Sage Risotto hot, garnished with chopped fresh sage leaves if desired.

Enjoy your delicious Pumpkin and Sage Risotto!

Wild Mushroom Risotto

Ingredients:

- 1 1/2 cups Arborio rice
- 4 cups vegetable or chicken broth
- 2 tablespoons olive oil
- 2 tablespoons unsalted butter
- 1 small onion, finely chopped
- 2 cloves garlic, minced
- 8 ounces mixed wild mushrooms (such as shiitake, cremini, and oyster), cleaned and sliced
- 1/2 cup dry white wine
- 1/4 cup grated Parmesan cheese
- Salt and pepper, to taste
- Fresh parsley, chopped (for garnish, optional)

Instructions:

1. In a small saucepan, heat the vegetable or chicken broth over low heat. Keep it warm while you prepare the risotto.
2. In a large skillet or saucepan, heat the olive oil and butter over medium heat. Add the chopped onion and cook until softened and translucent, about 5 minutes.
3. Add the minced garlic to the skillet and cook for an additional 1-2 minutes, until fragrant.
4. Add the sliced wild mushrooms to the skillet and cook for 5-7 minutes, or until they are tender and golden brown.
5. Add the Arborio rice to the skillet and cook for 1-2 minutes, stirring constantly, until the rice is well coated with the oil and butter.
6. Pour in the white wine and cook, stirring constantly, until the wine is absorbed by the rice.
7. Begin adding the warm broth to the skillet, one ladleful at a time, stirring constantly and allowing each addition of broth to be absorbed by the rice before adding more.
8. Continue adding broth and stirring until the rice is cooked through and creamy, but still slightly firm to the bite (al dente). This should take about 18-20 minutes.

9. Stir in the grated Parmesan cheese until melted and well incorporated. Season with salt and pepper to taste.
10. Remove the skillet from the heat and let the risotto rest for a minute or two before serving.
11. Serve the Wild Mushroom Risotto hot, garnished with chopped fresh parsley if desired.

Enjoy your delicious Wild Mushroom Risotto!

Broccoli and Blue Cheese Risotto

Ingredients:

- 1 1/2 cups Arborio rice
- 4 cups vegetable or chicken broth
- 2 tablespoons olive oil
- 2 tablespoons unsalted butter
- 1 small onion, finely chopped
- 2 cloves garlic, minced
- 2 cups broccoli florets, chopped into small pieces
- 1/2 cup dry white wine
- 1/2 cup crumbled blue cheese
- Salt and pepper, to taste
- Fresh parsley, chopped (for garnish, optional)

Instructions:

1. In a small saucepan, heat the vegetable or chicken broth over low heat. Keep it warm while you prepare the risotto.
2. In a large skillet or saucepan, heat the olive oil and butter over medium heat. Add the chopped onion and cook until softened and translucent, about 5 minutes.
3. Add the minced garlic to the skillet and cook for an additional 1-2 minutes, until fragrant.
4. Add the Arborio rice to the skillet and cook for 1-2 minutes, stirring constantly, until the rice is well coated with the oil and butter.
5. Pour in the white wine and cook, stirring constantly, until the wine is absorbed by the rice.
6. Begin adding the warm broth to the skillet, one ladleful at a time, stirring constantly and allowing each addition of broth to be absorbed by the rice before adding more.
7. About halfway through the cooking process (after about 10 minutes), stir in the chopped broccoli florets.
8. Continue adding broth and stirring until the rice is cooked through and creamy, but still slightly firm to the bite (al dente). This should take about 18-20 minutes.
9. Stir in the crumbled blue cheese until melted and well incorporated. Season with salt and pepper to taste.

10. Remove the skillet from the heat and let the risotto rest for a minute or two before serving.
11. Serve the Broccoli and Blue Cheese Risotto hot, garnished with chopped fresh parsley if desired.

Enjoy your delicious Broccoli and Blue Cheese Risotto!

Zucchini and Parmesan Risotto

Ingredients:

- 1 1/2 cups Arborio rice
- 4 cups vegetable or chicken broth
- 2 tablespoons olive oil
- 2 tablespoons unsalted butter
- 1 small onion, finely chopped
- 2 cloves garlic, minced
- 2 medium zucchinis, diced
- 1/2 cup dry white wine
- 1/2 cup grated Parmesan cheese
- Salt and pepper, to taste
- Fresh basil leaves, chopped (for garnish, optional)

Instructions:

1. In a small saucepan, heat the vegetable or chicken broth over low heat. Keep it warm while you prepare the risotto.
2. In a large skillet or saucepan, heat the olive oil and butter over medium heat. Add the chopped onion and cook until softened and translucent, about 5 minutes.
3. Add the minced garlic to the skillet and cook for an additional 1-2 minutes, until fragrant.
4. Add the diced zucchinis to the skillet and cook for 3-4 minutes, or until they are slightly softened.
5. Add the Arborio rice to the skillet and cook for 1-2 minutes, stirring constantly, until the rice is well coated with the oil and butter.
6. Pour in the white wine and cook, stirring constantly, until the wine is absorbed by the rice.
7. Begin adding the warm broth to the skillet, one ladleful at a time, stirring constantly and allowing each addition of broth to be absorbed by the rice before adding more.
8. Continue adding broth and stirring until the rice is cooked through and creamy, but still slightly firm to the bite (al dente). This should take about 18-20 minutes.
9. Stir in the grated Parmesan cheese until melted and well incorporated. Season with salt and pepper to taste.

10. Remove the skillet from the heat and let the risotto rest for a minute or two before serving.
11. Serve the Zucchini and Parmesan Risotto hot, garnished with chopped fresh basil leaves if desired.

Enjoy your delicious Zucchini and Parmesan Risotto!

Red Wine Risotto with Pancetta

Ingredients:

- 1 1/2 cups Arborio rice
- 4 cups chicken or vegetable broth
- 2 tablespoons olive oil
- 4 ounces pancetta, diced
- 1 small onion, finely chopped
- 2 cloves garlic, minced
- 1 cup red wine (choose a wine you enjoy drinking)
- 1/2 cup grated Parmesan cheese
- Salt and pepper, to taste
- Fresh parsley, chopped (for garnish, optional)

Instructions:

1. In a small saucepan, heat the chicken or vegetable broth over low heat. Keep it warm while you prepare the risotto.
2. In a large skillet or saucepan, heat the olive oil over medium heat. Add the diced pancetta and cook until crisp and golden brown, about 5-7 minutes. Remove the pancetta from the skillet and set aside, leaving the rendered fat in the skillet.
3. In the same skillet with the rendered fat, add the chopped onion and cook until softened and translucent, about 5 minutes.
4. Add the minced garlic to the skillet and cook for an additional 1-2 minutes, until fragrant.
5. Add the Arborio rice to the skillet and cook for 1-2 minutes, stirring constantly, until the rice is well coated with the oil and onions.
6. Pour in the red wine and cook, stirring constantly, until the wine is absorbed by the rice.
7. Begin adding the warm broth to the skillet, one ladleful at a time, stirring constantly and allowing each addition of broth to be absorbed by the rice before adding more.
8. Continue adding broth and stirring until the rice is cooked through and creamy, but still slightly firm to the bite (al dente). This should take about 18-20 minutes.
9. Stir in the grated Parmesan cheese until melted and well incorporated. Season with salt and pepper to taste.
10. Stir in the cooked pancetta.

11. Remove the skillet from the heat and let the risotto rest for a minute or two before serving.
12. Serve the Red Wine Risotto with Pancetta hot, garnished with chopped fresh parsley if desired.

Enjoy your delicious Red Wine Risotto with Pancetta!

Roasted Garlic Risotto

Ingredients:

- 1 1/2 cups Arborio rice
- 4 cups vegetable or chicken broth
- 1 head of garlic
- 2 tablespoons olive oil
- 2 tablespoons unsalted butter
- 1 small onion, finely chopped
- 1/2 cup dry white wine
- 1/4 cup grated Parmesan cheese
- Salt and pepper, to taste
- Fresh parsley, chopped (for garnish, optional)

Instructions:

1. Preheat your oven to 400°F (200°C).
2. Slice off the top of the head of garlic to expose the cloves. Place the garlic on a piece of aluminum foil, drizzle with olive oil, and wrap tightly in the foil. Roast in the preheated oven for 30-35 minutes, or until the garlic cloves are soft and golden brown. Remove from the oven and let cool.
3. Squeeze the roasted garlic cloves out of their skins into a small bowl. Use a fork to mash the garlic into a paste and set aside.
4. In a small saucepan, heat the vegetable or chicken broth over low heat. Keep it warm while you prepare the risotto.
5. In a large skillet or saucepan, heat the olive oil and butter over medium heat. Add the chopped onion and cook until softened and translucent, about 5 minutes.
6. Add the Arborio rice to the skillet and cook for 1-2 minutes, stirring constantly, until the rice is well coated with the oil and butter.
7. Pour in the white wine and cook, stirring constantly, until the wine is absorbed by the rice.
8. Begin adding the warm broth to the skillet, one ladleful at a time, stirring constantly and allowing each addition of broth to be absorbed by the rice before adding more.
9. Continue adding broth and stirring until the rice is cooked through and creamy, but still slightly firm to the bite (al dente). This should take about 18-20 minutes.

10. Stir in the mashed roasted garlic paste until well incorporated.
11. Stir in the grated Parmesan cheese until melted and well incorporated. Season with salt and pepper to taste.
12. Remove the skillet from the heat and let the risotto rest for a minute or two before serving.
13. Serve the Roasted Garlic Risotto hot, garnished with chopped fresh parsley if desired.

Enjoy your flavorful Roasted Garlic Risotto!

Smoked Salmon Risotto

Ingredients:

- 1 1/2 cups Arborio rice
- 4 cups vegetable or chicken broth
- 2 tablespoons olive oil
- 2 tablespoons unsalted butter
- 1 small onion, finely chopped
- 2 cloves garlic, minced
- 1/2 cup dry white wine
- 4 ounces smoked salmon, chopped into bite-sized pieces
- 1/4 cup grated Parmesan cheese
- Salt and pepper, to taste
- Fresh dill, chopped (for garnish, optional)
- Lemon wedges, for serving

Instructions:

1. In a small saucepan, heat the vegetable or chicken broth over low heat. Keep it warm while you prepare the risotto.
2. In a large skillet or saucepan, heat the olive oil and butter over medium heat. Add the chopped onion and cook until softened and translucent, about 5 minutes.
3. Add the minced garlic to the skillet and cook for an additional 1-2 minutes, until fragrant.
4. Add the Arborio rice to the skillet and cook for 1-2 minutes, stirring constantly, until the rice is well coated with the oil and butter.
5. Pour in the white wine and cook, stirring constantly, until the wine is absorbed by the rice.
6. Begin adding the warm broth to the skillet, one ladleful at a time, stirring constantly and allowing each addition of broth to be absorbed by the rice before adding more.
7. About halfway through the cooking process (after about 10 minutes), stir in the chopped smoked salmon.
8. Continue adding broth and stirring until the rice is cooked through and creamy, but still slightly firm to the bite (al dente). This should take about 18-20 minutes.

9. Stir in the grated Parmesan cheese until melted and well incorporated. Season with salt and pepper to taste.
10. Remove the skillet from the heat and let the risotto rest for a minute or two before serving.
11. Serve the Smoked Salmon Risotto hot, garnished with chopped fresh dill if desired, and lemon wedges on the side for squeezing over the risotto.

Enjoy your delicious Smoked Salmon Risotto!

Pesto Risotto with Cherry Tomatoes

Ingredients:

- 1 1/2 cups Arborio rice
- 4 cups vegetable or chicken broth
- 2 tablespoons olive oil
- 2 tablespoons unsalted butter
- 1 small onion, finely chopped
- 2 cloves garlic, minced
- 1/2 cup dry white wine
- 1/4 cup store-bought or homemade pesto sauce
- 1 cup cherry tomatoes, halved
- 1/4 cup grated Parmesan cheese
- Salt and pepper, to taste
- Fresh basil leaves, chopped (for garnish, optional)

Instructions:

1. In a small saucepan, heat the vegetable or chicken broth over low heat. Keep it warm while you prepare the risotto.
2. In a large skillet or saucepan, heat the olive oil and butter over medium heat. Add the chopped onion and cook until softened and translucent, about 5 minutes.
3. Add the minced garlic to the skillet and cook for an additional 1-2 minutes, until fragrant.
4. Add the Arborio rice to the skillet and cook for 1-2 minutes, stirring constantly, until the rice is well coated with the oil and butter.
5. Pour in the white wine and cook, stirring constantly, until the wine is absorbed by the rice.
6. Begin adding the warm broth to the skillet, one ladleful at a time, stirring constantly and allowing each addition of broth to be absorbed by the rice before adding more.
7. About halfway through the cooking process (after about 10 minutes), stir in the halved cherry tomatoes.
8. Continue adding broth and stirring until the rice is cooked through and creamy, but still slightly firm to the bite (al dente). This should take about 18-20 minutes.
9. Stir in the pesto sauce until well incorporated.

10. Stir in the grated Parmesan cheese until melted and well incorporated. Season with salt and pepper to taste.
11. Remove the skillet from the heat and let the risotto rest for a minute or two before serving.
12. Serve the Pesto Risotto with Cherry Tomatoes hot, garnished with chopped fresh basil leaves if desired.

Enjoy your delicious Pesto Risotto with Cherry Tomatoes!

Chicken and Sun-Dried Tomato Risotto

Ingredients:

- 1 1/2 cups Arborio rice
- 4 cups chicken broth
- 2 tablespoons olive oil
- 1 small onion, finely chopped
- 2 cloves garlic, minced
- 2 boneless, skinless chicken breasts, diced
- 1/2 cup dry white wine
- 1/2 cup sun-dried tomatoes, chopped
- 1/4 cup grated Parmesan cheese
- Salt and pepper, to taste
- Fresh basil leaves, chopped (for garnish, optional)

Instructions:

1. In a medium saucepan, heat the chicken broth over low heat. Keep it warm while you prepare the risotto.
2. In a large skillet or saucepan, heat the olive oil over medium heat. Add the chopped onion and cook until softened and translucent, about 5 minutes.
3. Add the minced garlic to the skillet and cook for an additional 1-2 minutes, until fragrant.
4. Add the diced chicken breasts to the skillet and cook until browned on all sides and cooked through, about 6-8 minutes.
5. Push the chicken to one side of the skillet and add the Arborio rice to the other side. Cook the rice for 1-2 minutes, stirring constantly, until it is well coated with the oil and onions.
6. Pour in the white wine and cook, stirring constantly, until the wine is absorbed by the rice.
7. Begin adding the warm chicken broth to the skillet, one ladleful at a time, stirring constantly and allowing each addition of broth to be absorbed by the rice before adding more.
8. About halfway through the cooking process (after about 10 minutes), stir in the chopped sun-dried tomatoes.

9. Continue adding broth and stirring until the rice is cooked through and creamy, but still slightly firm to the bite (al dente). This should take about 18-20 minutes.
10. Stir in the grated Parmesan cheese until melted and well incorporated. Season with salt and pepper to taste.
11. Remove the skillet from the heat and let the risotto rest for a minute or two before serving.
12. Serve the Chicken and Sun-Dried Tomato Risotto hot, garnished with chopped fresh basil leaves if desired.

Enjoy your delicious Chicken and Sun-Dried Tomato Risotto!

Fennel and Sausage Risotto

Ingredients:

- 1 1/2 cups Arborio rice
- 4 cups chicken or vegetable broth
- 2 tablespoons olive oil
- 1 small onion, finely chopped
- 2 cloves garlic, minced
- 2 Italian sausages, casings removed
- 1 fennel bulb, thinly sliced
- 1/2 cup dry white wine
- 1/4 cup grated Parmesan cheese
- Salt and pepper, to taste
- Fresh parsley, chopped (for garnish, optional)

Instructions:

1. In a medium saucepan, heat the chicken or vegetable broth over low heat. Keep it warm while you prepare the risotto.
2. In a large skillet or saucepan, heat the olive oil over medium heat. Add the chopped onion and cook until softened and translucent, about 5 minutes.
3. Add the minced garlic to the skillet and cook for an additional 1-2 minutes, until fragrant.
4. Add the Italian sausages to the skillet, breaking them up with a spoon, and cook until browned and cooked through, about 6-8 minutes.
5. Add the thinly sliced fennel to the skillet and cook for 5-7 minutes, or until the fennel is softened.
6. Push the sausage and fennel to one side of the skillet and add the Arborio rice to the other side. Cook the rice for 1-2 minutes, stirring constantly, until it is well coated with the oil and onions.
7. Pour in the white wine and cook, stirring constantly, until the wine is absorbed by the rice.
8. Begin adding the warm broth to the skillet, one ladleful at a time, stirring constantly and allowing each addition of broth to be absorbed by the rice before adding more.
9. Continue adding broth and stirring until the rice is cooked through and creamy, but still slightly firm to the bite (al dente). This should take about 18-20 minutes.

10. Stir in the grated Parmesan cheese until melted and well incorporated. Season with salt and pepper to taste.
11. Remove the skillet from the heat and let the risotto rest for a minute or two before serving.
12. Serve the Fennel and Sausage Risotto hot, garnished with chopped fresh parsley if desired.

Enjoy your delicious Fennel and Sausage Risotto!

Prosciutto and Pea Risotto

Ingredients:

- 1 1/2 cups Arborio rice
- 4 cups chicken or vegetable broth
- 2 tablespoons olive oil
- 1 small onion, finely chopped
- 2 cloves garlic, minced
- 4 slices prosciutto, chopped
- 1 cup frozen peas
- 1/2 cup dry white wine
- 1/4 cup grated Parmesan cheese
- Salt and pepper, to taste
- Fresh parsley, chopped (for garnish, optional)

Instructions:

1. In a medium saucepan, heat the chicken or vegetable broth over low heat. Keep it warm while you prepare the risotto.
2. In a large skillet or saucepan, heat the olive oil over medium heat. Add the chopped onion and cook until softened and translucent, about 5 minutes.
3. Add the minced garlic to the skillet and cook for an additional 1-2 minutes, until fragrant.
4. Add the chopped prosciutto to the skillet and cook until crisp, about 3-4 minutes.
5. Add the Arborio rice to the skillet and cook for 1-2 minutes, stirring constantly, until the rice is well coated with the oil and onions.
6. Pour in the white wine and cook, stirring constantly, until the wine is absorbed by the rice.
7. Begin adding the warm broth to the skillet, one ladleful at a time, stirring constantly and allowing each addition of broth to be absorbed by the rice before adding more.
8. About halfway through the cooking process (after about 10 minutes), stir in the frozen peas.
9. Continue adding broth and stirring until the rice is cooked through and creamy, but still slightly firm to the bite (al dente). This should take about 18-20 minutes.

10. Stir in the grated Parmesan cheese until melted and well incorporated. Season with salt and pepper to taste.
11. Remove the skillet from the heat and let the risotto rest for a minute or two before serving.
12. Serve the Prosciutto and Pea Risotto hot, garnished with chopped fresh parsley if desired.

Enjoy your delicious Prosciutto and Pea Risotto!

Cherry Tomato and Mozzarella Risotto

Ingredients:

- 1 1/2 cups Arborio rice
- 4 cups vegetable or chicken broth
- 2 tablespoons olive oil
- 1 small onion, finely chopped
- 2 cloves garlic, minced
- 1 cup cherry tomatoes, halved
- 1/2 cup dry white wine
- 1/2 cup shredded mozzarella cheese
- 1/4 cup grated Parmesan cheese
- Salt and pepper, to taste
- Fresh basil leaves, chopped (for garnish, optional)

Instructions:

1. In a medium saucepan, heat the vegetable or chicken broth over low heat. Keep it warm while you prepare the risotto.
2. In a large skillet or saucepan, heat the olive oil over medium heat. Add the chopped onion and cook until softened and translucent, about 5 minutes.
3. Add the minced garlic to the skillet and cook for an additional 1-2 minutes, until fragrant.
4. Add the Arborio rice to the skillet and cook for 1-2 minutes, stirring constantly, until the rice is well coated with the oil and onions.
5. Pour in the white wine and cook, stirring constantly, until the wine is absorbed by the rice.
6. Begin adding the warm broth to the skillet, one ladleful at a time, stirring constantly and allowing each addition of broth to be absorbed by the rice before adding more.
7. About halfway through the cooking process (after about 10 minutes), stir in the halved cherry tomatoes.
8. Continue adding broth and stirring until the rice is cooked through and creamy, but still slightly firm to the bite (al dente). This should take about 18-20 minutes.
9. Stir in the shredded mozzarella cheese until melted and well incorporated.

10. Stir in the grated Parmesan cheese until melted and well incorporated. Season with salt and pepper to taste.
11. Remove the skillet from the heat and let the risotto rest for a minute or two before serving.
12. Serve the Cherry Tomato and Mozzarella Risotto hot, garnished with chopped fresh basil leaves if desired.

Enjoy your delicious Cherry Tomato and Mozzarella Risotto!

Butternut Squash and Sage Risotto

Ingredients:

- 1 small butternut squash, peeled, seeded, and diced
- 4 cups vegetable or chicken broth
- 2 tablespoons olive oil
- 1 small onion, finely chopped
- 2 cloves garlic, minced
- 1 1/2 cups Arborio rice
- 1/2 cup dry white wine
- 2 tablespoons fresh sage, finely chopped
- 1/4 cup grated Parmesan cheese
- Salt and pepper, to taste
- Fresh sage leaves, for garnish (optional)

Instructions:

1. Preheat your oven to 400°F (200°C). Place the diced butternut squash on a baking sheet lined with parchment paper. Drizzle with olive oil, season with salt and pepper, and toss to coat. Roast in the preheated oven for 20-25 minutes, or until the squash is tender and lightly caramelized. Remove from the oven and set aside.
2. In a medium saucepan, heat the vegetable or chicken broth over low heat. Keep it warm while you prepare the risotto.
3. In a large skillet or saucepan, heat the olive oil over medium heat. Add the chopped onion and cook until softened and translucent, about 5 minutes.
4. Add the minced garlic to the skillet and cook for an additional 1-2 minutes, until fragrant.
5. Add the Arborio rice to the skillet and cook for 1-2 minutes, stirring constantly, until the rice is well coated with the oil and onions.
6. Pour in the white wine and cook, stirring constantly, until the wine is absorbed by the rice.
7. Begin adding the warm broth to the skillet, one ladleful at a time, stirring constantly and allowing each addition of broth to be absorbed by the rice before adding more.
8. About halfway through the cooking process (after about 10 minutes), stir in the roasted butternut squash and chopped sage.

9. Continue adding broth and stirring until the rice is cooked through and creamy, but still slightly firm to the bite (al dente). This should take about 18-20 minutes.
10. Stir in the grated Parmesan cheese until melted and well incorporated. Season with salt and pepper to taste.
11. Remove the skillet from the heat and let the risotto rest for a minute or two before serving.
12. Serve the Butternut Squash and Sage Risotto hot, garnished with fresh sage leaves if desired.

Enjoy your delicious Butternut Squash and Sage Risotto!

Pancetta and Leek Risotto

Ingredients:

- 1 1/2 cups Arborio rice
- 4 cups chicken or vegetable broth
- 2 tablespoons olive oil
- 4 ounces pancetta, diced
- 2 leeks, white and light green parts only, thinly sliced
- 2 cloves garlic, minced
- 1/2 cup dry white wine
- 1/4 cup grated Parmesan cheese
- Salt and pepper, to taste
- Fresh parsley, chopped (for garnish, optional)

Instructions:

1. In a medium saucepan, heat the chicken or vegetable broth over low heat. Keep it warm while you prepare the risotto.
2. In a large skillet or saucepan, heat the olive oil over medium heat. Add the diced pancetta and cook until crispy, about 5 minutes.
3. Remove the cooked pancetta from the skillet and set aside. Leave the rendered fat in the skillet.
4. Add the thinly sliced leeks to the skillet and cook until softened, about 5 minutes.
5. Add the minced garlic to the skillet and cook for an additional 1-2 minutes, until fragrant.
6. Add the Arborio rice to the skillet and cook for 1-2 minutes, stirring constantly, until the rice is well coated with the fat and leeks.
7. Pour in the white wine and cook, stirring constantly, until the wine is absorbed by the rice.
8. Begin adding the warm broth to the skillet, one ladleful at a time, stirring constantly and allowing each addition of broth to be absorbed by the rice before adding more.
9. About halfway through the cooking process (after about 10 minutes), stir in the cooked pancetta.
10. Continue adding broth and stirring until the rice is cooked through and creamy, but still slightly firm to the bite (al dente). This should take about 18-20 minutes.

11. Stir in the grated Parmesan cheese until melted and well incorporated. Season with salt and pepper to taste.
12. Remove the skillet from the heat and let the risotto rest for a minute or two before serving.
13. Serve the Pancetta and Leek Risotto hot, garnished with chopped fresh parsley if desired.

Enjoy your delicious Pancetta and Leek Risotto!

Roasted Vegetable Risotto

Ingredients:

- 1 cup Arborio rice
- 4 cups vegetable broth
- 2 tablespoons olive oil
- 1 small onion, finely chopped
- 2 cloves garlic, minced
- Assorted vegetables (such as bell peppers, zucchini, cherry tomatoes, mushrooms, carrots, etc.), diced or sliced
- Salt and pepper, to taste
- Grated Parmesan cheese, for serving (optional)
- Fresh herbs (such as basil, parsley, or thyme), for garnish (optional)

Instructions:

1. Preheat your oven to 400°F (200°C). Place the diced or sliced vegetables on a baking sheet lined with parchment paper. Drizzle with olive oil, season with salt and pepper, and toss to coat. Roast in the preheated oven for 20-25 minutes, or until the vegetables are tender and lightly caramelized. Remove from the oven and set aside.
2. In a medium saucepan, heat the vegetable broth over low heat. Keep it warm while you prepare the risotto.
3. In a large skillet or saucepan, heat the olive oil over medium heat. Add the chopped onion and cook until softened and translucent, about 5 minutes.
4. Add the minced garlic to the skillet and cook for an additional 1-2 minutes, until fragrant.
5. Add the Arborio rice to the skillet and cook for 1-2 minutes, stirring constantly, until the rice is well coated with the oil and onions.
6. Pour in a ladleful of warm vegetable broth and cook, stirring constantly, until the broth is absorbed by the rice.
7. Continue adding the warm broth to the skillet, one ladleful at a time, stirring constantly and allowing each addition of broth to be absorbed by the rice before adding more. This process will take about 18-20 minutes.
8. About halfway through the cooking process (after about 10 minutes), stir in the roasted vegetables.

9. Continue adding broth and stirring until the rice is cooked through and creamy, but still slightly firm to the bite (al dente).
10. Once the risotto is cooked, remove the skillet from the heat. Season with additional salt and pepper if needed.
11. Serve the Roasted Vegetable Risotto hot, garnished with grated Parmesan cheese and fresh herbs if desired.

Enjoy your delicious Roasted Vegetable Risotto!

Spinach and Feta Risotto

Ingredients:

- 1 cup Arborio rice
- 4 cups vegetable or chicken broth
- 2 tablespoons olive oil
- 1 small onion, finely chopped
- 2 cloves garlic, minced
- 4 cups fresh spinach, chopped
- 1/2 cup crumbled feta cheese
- Salt and pepper, to taste
- Grated Parmesan cheese, for serving (optional)
- Fresh parsley, chopped, for garnish (optional)

Instructions:

1. In a medium saucepan, heat the vegetable or chicken broth over low heat. Keep it warm while you prepare the risotto.
2. In a large skillet or saucepan, heat the olive oil over medium heat. Add the chopped onion and cook until softened and translucent, about 5 minutes.
3. Add the minced garlic to the skillet and cook for an additional 1-2 minutes, until fragrant.
4. Add the Arborio rice to the skillet and cook for 1-2 minutes, stirring constantly, until the rice is well coated with the oil and onions.
5. Pour in a ladleful of warm broth and cook, stirring constantly, until the broth is absorbed by the rice.
6. Continue adding the warm broth to the skillet, one ladleful at a time, stirring constantly and allowing each addition of broth to be absorbed by the rice before adding more. This process will take about 18-20 minutes.
7. About halfway through the cooking process (after about 10 minutes), stir in the chopped spinach.
8. Continue adding broth and stirring until the rice is cooked through and creamy, but still slightly firm to the bite (al dente).
9. Once the risotto is cooked, remove the skillet from the heat. Stir in the crumbled feta cheese until it's melted and well incorporated into the risotto. Season with salt and pepper to taste.

10. Serve the Spinach and Feta Risotto hot, garnished with grated Parmesan cheese and fresh parsley if desired.

Enjoy your delicious Spinach and Feta Risotto!

Roasted Butternut Squash Risotto

Ingredients:

- 1 small butternut squash, peeled, seeded, and diced
- 2 tablespoons olive oil
- Salt and pepper, to taste
- 4 cups vegetable or chicken broth
- 1 tablespoon butter
- 1 small onion, finely chopped
- 2 cloves garlic, minced
- 1 1/2 cups Arborio rice
- 1/2 cup dry white wine (optional)
- 1/2 cup grated Parmesan cheese
- Fresh parsley or sage, chopped (for garnish)

Instructions:

1. Preheat your oven to 400°F (200°C). Place the diced butternut squash on a baking sheet lined with parchment paper. Drizzle with olive oil, season with salt and pepper, and toss to coat. Roast in the preheated oven for 25-30 minutes, or until the squash is tender and lightly caramelized. Remove from the oven and set aside.
2. In a medium saucepan, heat the vegetable or chicken broth over low heat. Keep it warm while you prepare the risotto.
3. In a large skillet or saucepan, melt the butter over medium heat. Add the chopped onion and cook until softened, about 5 minutes. Add the minced garlic and cook for an additional minute.
4. Add the Arborio rice to the skillet and cook for 1-2 minutes, stirring constantly, until the rice is well coated with the butter and onions.
5. If using, pour in the white wine and cook until it is mostly absorbed by the rice.
6. Begin adding the warm broth to the skillet, one ladleful at a time, stirring constantly and allowing each addition of broth to be absorbed by the rice before adding more.
7. Continue adding broth and stirring until the rice is creamy and cooked al dente, about 18-20 minutes.

8. Stir in the roasted butternut squash and grated Parmesan cheese until well combined. Season with additional salt and pepper to taste.
9. Remove the skillet from the heat and let the risotto rest for a minute or two.
10. Serve the Roasted Butternut Squash Risotto hot, garnished with chopped parsley or sage.

Enjoy your delicious Roasted Butternut Squash Risotto!

Porcini and Thyme Risotto

Ingredients:

- 1 cup Arborio rice
- 4 cups vegetable or chicken broth
- 1 ounce dried porcini mushrooms
- 2 tablespoons olive oil
- 1 small onion, finely chopped
- 2 cloves garlic, minced
- 1/2 cup dry white wine
- 1 tablespoon fresh thyme leaves
- 1/4 cup grated Parmesan cheese
- Salt and pepper, to taste
- Fresh thyme sprigs, for garnish (optional)

Instructions:

1. In a medium saucepan, heat the vegetable or chicken broth over low heat. Add the dried porcini mushrooms to the broth and let them soak for about 15-20 minutes, until softened. Remove the mushrooms from the broth, chop them into small pieces, and set aside. Keep the broth warm.
2. In a large skillet or saucepan, heat the olive oil over medium heat. Add the chopped onion and cook until softened and translucent, about 5 minutes.
3. Add the minced garlic to the skillet and cook for an additional 1-2 minutes, until fragrant.
4. Add the Arborio rice to the skillet and cook for 1-2 minutes, stirring constantly, until the rice is well coated with the oil and onions.
5. Pour in the white wine and cook, stirring constantly, until the wine is absorbed by the rice.
6. Begin adding the warm broth to the skillet, one ladleful at a time, stirring constantly and allowing each addition of broth to be absorbed by the rice before adding more.
7. About halfway through the cooking process (after about 10 minutes), stir in the chopped porcini mushrooms and fresh thyme leaves.
8. Continue adding broth and stirring until the rice is cooked through and creamy, but still slightly firm to the bite (al dente). This should take about 18-20 minutes.

9. Stir in the grated Parmesan cheese until melted and well incorporated. Season with salt and pepper to taste.
10. Remove the skillet from the heat and let the risotto rest for a minute or two before serving.
11. Serve the Porcini and Thyme Risotto hot, garnished with fresh thyme sprigs if desired.

Enjoy your delicious Porcini and Thyme Risotto!

Zucchini Blossom Risotto

Ingredients:

- 1 cup Arborio rice
- 4 cups vegetable or chicken broth
- 2 tablespoons olive oil
- 1 small onion, finely chopped
- 2 cloves garlic, minced
- 1/2 cup dry white wine (optional)
- 1/2 cup grated Parmesan cheese
- Salt and pepper, to taste
- 6-8 zucchini blossoms, stamens removed and petals chopped
- Zest of 1 lemon (optional)
- Fresh basil or parsley, chopped, for garnish

Instructions:

1. In a medium saucepan, heat the vegetable or chicken broth over low heat. Keep it warm while you prepare the risotto.
2. In a large skillet or saucepan, heat the olive oil over medium heat. Add the chopped onion and cook until softened and translucent, about 5 minutes.
3. Add the minced garlic to the skillet and cook for an additional 1-2 minutes, until fragrant.
4. Add the Arborio rice to the skillet and cook for 1-2 minutes, stirring constantly, until the rice is well coated with the oil and onions.
5. If using, pour in the white wine and cook until it is mostly absorbed by the rice.
6. Begin adding the warm broth to the skillet, one ladleful at a time, stirring constantly and allowing each addition of broth to be absorbed by the rice before adding more.
7. About halfway through the cooking process (after about 10 minutes), stir in the chopped zucchini blossoms.
8. Continue adding broth and stirring until the rice is creamy and cooked al dente, about 18-20 minutes.
9. Once the risotto is cooked, remove the skillet from the heat. Stir in the grated Parmesan cheese until it's melted and well incorporated into the risotto. Season with salt and pepper to taste.
10. If using, stir in the lemon zest for a fresh citrusy flavor.

11. Serve the Zucchini Blossom Risotto hot, garnished with chopped fresh basil or parsley.

Enjoy your delicate and flavorful Zucchini Blossom Risotto!

Roasted Beet Risotto with Goat Cheese

Ingredients:

- 1 cup Arborio rice
- 4 cups vegetable or chicken broth
- 2 tablespoons olive oil
- 1 small onion, finely chopped
- 2 cloves garlic, minced
- 2 medium-sized beets, roasted, peeled, and diced
- 2 ounces goat cheese, crumbled
- Salt and pepper, to taste
- 2 tablespoons chopped fresh parsley, for garnish (optional)

Instructions:

1. Preheat your oven to 400°F (200°C). Wrap the beets individually in aluminum foil and roast them in the oven for about 45-60 minutes, or until they are tender when pierced with a fork. Once roasted, let them cool slightly, then peel and dice them into small cubes.
2. In a medium saucepan, heat the vegetable or chicken broth over low heat. Keep it warm while you prepare the risotto.
3. In a large skillet or saucepan, heat the olive oil over medium heat. Add the chopped onion and cook until softened and translucent, about 5 minutes.
4. Add the minced garlic to the skillet and cook for an additional 1-2 minutes, until fragrant.
5. Add the Arborio rice to the skillet and cook for 1-2 minutes, stirring constantly, until the rice is well coated with the oil and onions.
6. Begin adding the warm broth to the skillet, one ladleful at a time, stirring constantly and allowing each addition of broth to be absorbed by the rice before adding more.
7. About halfway through the cooking process (after about 10 minutes), stir in the diced roasted beets.
8. Continue adding broth and stirring until the rice is cooked through and creamy, but still slightly firm to the bite (al dente). This should take about 18-20 minutes.
9. Once the risotto is cooked, remove the skillet from the heat. Stir in the crumbled goat cheese until it's melted and well incorporated into the risotto. Season with salt and pepper to taste.

10. Serve the Roasted Beet Risotto with Goat Cheese hot, garnished with chopped fresh parsley if desired.

Enjoy your vibrant and delicious Roasted Beet Risotto with Goat Cheese!

Lemon and Parmesan Risotto

Ingredients:

- 1 cup Arborio rice
- 4 cups vegetable or chicken broth
- 2 tablespoons olive oil
- 1 small onion, finely chopped
- 2 cloves garlic, minced
- Zest and juice of 1 lemon
- 1/2 cup dry white wine (optional)
- 1/2 cup grated Parmesan cheese
- Salt and pepper, to taste
- Fresh parsley or basil, chopped, for garnish (optional)

Instructions:

1. In a medium saucepan, heat the vegetable or chicken broth over low heat. Keep it warm while you prepare the risotto.
2. In a large skillet or saucepan, heat the olive oil over medium heat. Add the chopped onion and cook until softened and translucent, about 5 minutes.
3. Add the minced garlic to the skillet and cook for an additional 1-2 minutes, until fragrant.
4. Add the Arborio rice to the skillet and cook for 1-2 minutes, stirring constantly, until the rice is well coated with the oil and onions.
5. If using, pour in the white wine and cook until it is mostly absorbed by the rice.
6. Begin adding the warm broth to the skillet, one ladleful at a time, stirring constantly and allowing each addition of broth to be absorbed by the rice before adding more.
7. About halfway through the cooking process (after about 10 minutes), stir in the lemon zest and juice.
8. Continue adding broth and stirring until the rice is creamy and cooked al dente, about 18-20 minutes.
9. Once the risotto is cooked, remove the skillet from the heat. Stir in the grated Parmesan cheese until it's melted and well incorporated into the risotto. Season with salt and pepper to taste.

10. Serve the Lemon and Parmesan Risotto hot, garnished with chopped fresh parsley or basil if desired.

Enjoy your creamy and flavorful Lemon and Parmesan Risotto!

Mushroom and Leek Risotto

Ingredients:

- 1 cup Arborio rice
- 4 cups vegetable or chicken broth
- 2 tablespoons olive oil
- 1 small onion, finely chopped
- 2 cloves garlic, minced
- 8 ounces mushrooms (such as cremini or button), sliced
- 2 leeks, white and light green parts only, thinly sliced
- 1/2 cup dry white wine (optional)
- 1/2 cup grated Parmesan cheese
- Salt and pepper, to taste
- Fresh parsley, chopped, for garnish (optional)

Instructions:

1. In a medium saucepan, heat the vegetable or chicken broth over low heat. Keep it warm while you prepare the risotto.
2. In a large skillet or saucepan, heat the olive oil over medium heat. Add the chopped onion and cook until softened and translucent, about 5 minutes.
3. Add the minced garlic to the skillet and cook for an additional 1-2 minutes, until fragrant.
4. Add the sliced mushrooms to the skillet and cook until they release their moisture and become golden brown, about 8-10 minutes.
5. Add the thinly sliced leeks to the skillet and cook until softened, about 5 minutes.
6. Add the Arborio rice to the skillet and cook for 1-2 minutes, stirring constantly, until the rice is well coated with the oil and vegetables.
7. If using, pour in the white wine and cook until it is mostly absorbed by the rice.
8. Begin adding the warm broth to the skillet, one ladleful at a time, stirring constantly and allowing each addition of broth to be absorbed by the rice before adding more.
9. Continue adding broth and stirring until the rice is creamy and cooked al dente, about 18-20 minutes.

10. Once the risotto is cooked, remove the skillet from the heat. Stir in the grated Parmesan cheese until it's melted and well incorporated into the risotto. Season with salt and pepper to taste.
11. Serve the Mushroom and Leek Risotto hot, garnished with chopped fresh parsley if desired.

Enjoy your delicious Mushroom and Leek Risotto!

Smoked Gouda and Asparagus Risotto

Ingredients:

- 1 cup Arborio rice
- 4 cups vegetable or chicken broth
- 2 tablespoons olive oil
- 1 small onion, finely chopped
- 2 cloves garlic, minced
- 1/2 cup dry white wine (optional)
- 1 bunch asparagus, trimmed and cut into bite-sized pieces
- 4 ounces smoked Gouda cheese, grated
- Salt and pepper, to taste
- Fresh parsley, chopped, for garnish (optional)

Instructions:

1. In a medium saucepan, heat the vegetable or chicken broth over low heat. Keep it warm while you prepare the risotto.
2. In a large skillet or saucepan, heat the olive oil over medium heat. Add the chopped onion and cook until softened and translucent, about 5 minutes.
3. Add the minced garlic to the skillet and cook for an additional 1-2 minutes, until fragrant.
4. Add the Arborio rice to the skillet and cook for 1-2 minutes, stirring constantly, until the rice is well coated with the oil and onions.
5. If using, pour in the white wine and cook until it is mostly absorbed by the rice.
6. Begin adding the warm broth to the skillet, one ladleful at a time, stirring constantly and allowing each addition of broth to be absorbed by the rice before adding more.
7. About halfway through the cooking process (after about 10 minutes), stir in the bite-sized pieces of asparagus.
8. Continue adding broth and stirring until the rice is creamy and cooked al dente, about 18-20 minutes.
9. Once the risotto is cooked, remove the skillet from the heat. Stir in the grated smoked Gouda cheese until it's melted and well incorporated into the risotto. Season with salt and pepper to taste.

10. Serve the Smoked Gouda and Asparagus Risotto hot, garnished with chopped fresh parsley if desired.

Enjoy your delicious Smoked Gouda and Asparagus Risotto!

Sun-Dried Tomato and Basil Risotto

Ingredients:

- 1 cup Arborio rice
- 4 cups vegetable or chicken broth
- 2 tablespoons olive oil
- 1 small onion, finely chopped
- 2 cloves garlic, minced
- 1/2 cup dry white wine (optional)
- 1/2 cup sun-dried tomatoes, chopped
- 1/4 cup fresh basil leaves, chopped
- 1/2 cup grated Parmesan cheese
- Salt and pepper, to taste

Instructions:

1. In a medium saucepan, heat the vegetable or chicken broth over low heat. Keep it warm while you prepare the risotto.
2. In a large skillet or saucepan, heat the olive oil over medium heat. Add the chopped onion and cook until softened and translucent, about 5 minutes.
3. Add the minced garlic to the skillet and cook for an additional 1-2 minutes, until fragrant.
4. Add the Arborio rice to the skillet and cook for 1-2 minutes, stirring constantly, until the rice is well coated with the oil and onions.
5. If using, pour in the white wine and cook until it is mostly absorbed by the rice.
6. Begin adding the warm broth to the skillet, one ladleful at a time, stirring constantly and allowing each addition of broth to be absorbed by the rice before adding more.
7. About halfway through the cooking process (after about 10 minutes), stir in the chopped sun-dried tomatoes.
8. Continue adding broth and stirring until the rice is creamy and cooked al dente, about 18-20 minutes.
9. Once the risotto is cooked, remove the skillet from the heat. Stir in the chopped fresh basil and grated Parmesan cheese until they're well incorporated into the risotto. Season with salt and pepper to taste.

10. Serve the Sun-Dried Tomato and Basil Risotto hot, garnished with additional chopped basil leaves if desired.

Enjoy your flavorful Sun-Dried Tomato and Basil Risotto!

Cherry Tomato and Basil Risotto

Ingredients:

- 1 cup Arborio rice
- 4 cups vegetable or chicken broth
- 2 tablespoons olive oil
- 1 small onion, finely chopped
- 2 cloves garlic, minced
- 1/2 cup dry white wine (optional)
- 1 pint cherry tomatoes, halved
- 1/4 cup fresh basil leaves, chopped
- 1/2 cup grated Parmesan cheese
- Salt and pepper, to taste

Instructions:

1. In a medium saucepan, heat the vegetable or chicken broth over low heat. Keep it warm while you prepare the risotto.
2. In a large skillet or saucepan, heat the olive oil over medium heat. Add the chopped onion and cook until softened and translucent, about 5 minutes.
3. Add the minced garlic to the skillet and cook for an additional 1-2 minutes, until fragrant.
4. Add the Arborio rice to the skillet and cook for 1-2 minutes, stirring constantly, until the rice is well coated with the oil and onions.
5. If using, pour in the white wine and cook until it is mostly absorbed by the rice.
6. Begin adding the warm broth to the skillet, one ladleful at a time, stirring constantly and allowing each addition of broth to be absorbed by the rice before adding more.
7. About halfway through the cooking process (after about 10 minutes), stir in the halved cherry tomatoes.
8. Continue adding broth and stirring until the rice is creamy and cooked al dente, about 18-20 minutes.
9. Once the risotto is cooked, remove the skillet from the heat. Stir in the chopped fresh basil and grated Parmesan cheese until they're well incorporated into the risotto. Season with salt and pepper to taste.

10. Serve the Cherry Tomato and Basil Risotto hot, garnished with additional chopped basil leaves if desired.

Enjoy your fresh and flavorful Cherry Tomato and Basil Risotto!

Pancetta and Mushroom Risotto

Ingredients:

- 1 cup Arborio rice
- 4 cups vegetable or chicken broth
- 2 tablespoons olive oil
- 4 ounces pancetta, diced
- 8 ounces mushrooms (such as cremini or button), sliced
- 1 small onion, finely chopped
- 2 cloves garlic, minced
- 1/2 cup dry white wine (optional)
- 1/2 cup grated Parmesan cheese
- Salt and pepper, to taste
- Fresh parsley, chopped, for garnish (optional)

Instructions:

1. In a medium saucepan, heat the vegetable or chicken broth over low heat. Keep it warm while you prepare the risotto.
2. In a large skillet or saucepan, heat the olive oil over medium heat. Add the diced pancetta and cook until crispy and golden brown, about 5-7 minutes. Remove the pancetta from the skillet and set aside, leaving the rendered fat in the skillet.
3. In the same skillet, add the sliced mushrooms and cook until they release their moisture and become golden brown, about 8-10 minutes. Remove the mushrooms from the skillet and set aside.
4. Add the chopped onion to the skillet and cook until softened and translucent, about 5 minutes.
5. Add the minced garlic to the skillet and cook for an additional 1-2 minutes, until fragrant.
6. Add the Arborio rice to the skillet and cook for 1-2 minutes, stirring constantly, until the rice is well coated with the oil and onions.
7. If using, pour in the white wine and cook until it is mostly absorbed by the rice.
8. Begin adding the warm broth to the skillet, one ladleful at a time, stirring constantly and allowing each addition of broth to be absorbed by the rice before adding more.

9. About halfway through the cooking process (after about 10 minutes), stir in the cooked pancetta and mushrooms.
10. Continue adding broth and stirring until the rice is creamy and cooked al dente, about 18-20 minutes.
11. Once the risotto is cooked, remove the skillet from the heat. Stir in the grated Parmesan cheese until it's melted and well incorporated into the risotto. Season with salt and pepper to taste.
12. Serve the Pancetta and Mushroom Risotto hot, garnished with chopped fresh parsley if desired.

Enjoy your delicious Pancetta and Mushroom Risotto!

Crab and Asparagus Risotto

Ingredients:

- 1 cup Arborio rice
- 4 cups vegetable or chicken broth
- 2 tablespoons olive oil
- 1 small onion, finely chopped
- 2 cloves garlic, minced
- 1/2 cup dry white wine (optional)
- 8 ounces lump crab meat
- 1 bunch asparagus, trimmed and cut into bite-sized pieces
- 1/2 cup grated Parmesan cheese
- Salt and pepper, to taste
- Fresh parsley, chopped, for garnish (optional)
- Lemon wedges, for serving

Instructions:

1. In a medium saucepan, heat the vegetable or chicken broth over low heat. Keep it warm while you prepare the risotto.
2. In a large skillet or saucepan, heat the olive oil over medium heat. Add the chopped onion and cook until softened and translucent, about 5 minutes.
3. Add the minced garlic to the skillet and cook for an additional 1-2 minutes, until fragrant.
4. Add the Arborio rice to the skillet and cook for 1-2 minutes, stirring constantly, until the rice is well coated with the oil and onions.
5. If using, pour in the white wine and cook until it is mostly absorbed by the rice.
6. Begin adding the warm broth to the skillet, one ladleful at a time, stirring constantly and allowing each addition of broth to be absorbed by the rice before adding more.
7. About halfway through the cooking process (after about 10 minutes), stir in the bite-sized pieces of asparagus.
8. Continue adding broth and stirring until the rice is creamy and cooked al dente, about 18-20 minutes.

9. Once the risotto is cooked, remove the skillet from the heat. Stir in the lump crab meat and grated Parmesan cheese until they're well incorporated into the risotto. Season with salt and pepper to taste.
10. Serve the Crab and Asparagus Risotto hot, garnished with chopped fresh parsley if desired. Serve with lemon wedges on the side for squeezing over the risotto.

Enjoy your luxurious Crab and Asparagus Risotto!

Roasted Eggplant Risotto

Ingredients:

- 1 medium eggplant, diced into small cubes
- 2 tablespoons olive oil
- Salt and pepper, to taste
- 1 cup Arborio rice
- 4 cups vegetable or chicken broth
- 1 small onion, finely chopped
- 2 cloves garlic, minced
- 1/2 cup dry white wine (optional)
- 1/2 cup grated Parmesan cheese
- Fresh basil leaves, chopped, for garnish (optional)

Instructions:

1. Preheat your oven to 400°F (200°C). Place the diced eggplant on a baking sheet and drizzle with olive oil. Season with salt and pepper to taste. Toss to coat evenly. Roast in the preheated oven for about 20-25 minutes, or until the eggplant is tender and golden brown. Remove from the oven and set aside.
2. In a medium saucepan, heat the vegetable or chicken broth over low heat. Keep it warm while you prepare the risotto.
3. In a large skillet or saucepan, heat the olive oil over medium heat. Add the chopped onion and cook until softened and translucent, about 5 minutes.
4. Add the minced garlic to the skillet and cook for an additional 1-2 minutes, until fragrant.
5. Add the Arborio rice to the skillet and cook for 1-2 minutes, stirring constantly, until the rice is well coated with the oil and onions.
6. If using, pour in the white wine and cook until it is mostly absorbed by the rice.
7. Begin adding the warm broth to the skillet, one ladleful at a time, stirring constantly and allowing each addition of broth to be absorbed by the rice before adding more.
8. About halfway through the cooking process (after about 10 minutes), stir in the roasted eggplant.
9. Continue adding broth and stirring until the rice is creamy and cooked al dente, about 18-20 minutes.

10. Once the risotto is cooked, remove the skillet from the heat. Stir in the grated Parmesan cheese until it's melted and well incorporated into the risotto. Season with salt and pepper to taste.
11. Serve the Roasted Eggplant Risotto hot, garnished with chopped fresh basil leaves if desired.

Enjoy your creamy and delicious Roasted Eggplant Risotto!

Creamy Parmesan Risotto

Ingredients:

- 1 ½ cups Arborio rice
- 4 cups chicken or vegetable broth
- 1 cup grated Parmesan cheese
- 1 small onion, finely chopped
- 2 cloves garlic, minced
- ½ cup dry white wine
- 2 tablespoons unsalted butter
- 2 tablespoons olive oil
- Salt and pepper to taste
- Fresh chopped parsley (for garnish, optional)

Instructions:

1. Prepare the Broth: In a saucepan, heat the broth over low heat until warm. Keep it simmering while you prepare the risotto.
2. Sauté Onions and Garlic: In a large, heavy-bottomed skillet or pot, heat the olive oil and butter over medium heat. Add the chopped onion and garlic, and sauté until softened and translucent, about 3-4 minutes.
3. Toast the Rice: Add the Arborio rice to the skillet with the onions and garlic. Stir to coat the rice with the oil and butter mixture. Cook for 1-2 minutes, until the rice becomes slightly translucent around the edges.
4. Deglaze with Wine: Pour in the white wine and stir constantly until it's absorbed by the rice.
5. Add Broth: Begin adding the warm broth to the rice mixture, one ladleful at a time, stirring frequently. Allow each addition of broth to be absorbed by the rice before adding more. Continue this process until the rice is creamy and tender, but still slightly firm to the bite. This typically takes about 18-20 minutes.
6. Finish with Parmesan: Once the rice is cooked to your desired consistency, remove the skillet from the heat. Stir in the grated Parmesan cheese until it's melted and incorporated into the risotto. Season with salt and pepper to taste.
7. Serve: Transfer the risotto to serving plates or bowls. Garnish with chopped parsley if desired. Serve hot, and enjoy!

Risotto is best enjoyed immediately while it's still creamy and hot. If you have any leftovers, you can store them in an airtight container in the refrigerator for up to 2 days, but keep in mind that the texture may change upon reheating.

Printed in the USA
CPSIA information can be obtained
at www.ICGtesting.com
CBHW080533020824
12556CB00050B/1007